EXPRESSIONS 2

A Book of Poetic Thoughts

MARIO GIVENS

EXPRESSIONS 2

Copyright © 2023 by Mario Givens

All rights reserved. No part of this book maybe reproduced or transmitted in any form or by any means without prior written permission from the author.

ISBN: 978-1-953638-56-4
LCCN: 2023904185

Printed in the United States of America

This book or parts thereof may not be reproduced in any form, stored in a retrieval system, or transmitted in any form by any means-electronic, mechanical, photocopy, recording, or otherwise- without prior written permission of the publisher, except as provided by United States of America copyright law.

PUBLISHER | TA MEDIA CO
WWW.PUBLISHYOURBOOKTODAY.INFO
WWW.PUBLISHWITHTIFFANY.COM

Acknowledgments

I would like to say all praises are due to God for making it all possible for me to write this book. In addition to Tiffany A Green and TA Media +Co for providing the resources to make my vision clear so the readers can enjoy my thoughts. The path we've taken to get to this point in our lives has been refreshing and rewarding.

Dedication

To my children Nia and Mario jr. thank you for being the rock to my soul. To Lorenzo Allen thank you for telling me to take my time and there's no rush to finishing this book. I want to thank everyone who supported me and my other past writings. May God bless you all.

Introduction

In this book there will be truths to many events that happen in my life past and present. My writing style comes with a different delivery with poetry that tells short stories and i use symbolism as a way to keep the readers engaged.

Table of Contents

Heart of Concrete 1

Death of a Gentleman 2

Black Cloud 4

A Jazzy Thought 5

I Just Made Love to You Invisibly 6

A Seasonal Purpose 8

A Destroyed Promise 10

Phenomenal Soul 12

A Thoughtful Date 14

Lifeless Love 16

Ear Trumpet 17

Wings 18

A Warm Jamaican Moment 19

Sage 20

Her 21

A Perfect DAY 22

One Night Understand 23

A Deep Cleaning 25

Table 26

Death of a Poet	27
Dark Light	28
Heaven Sent	30
Lay	31
Forgive	32
Missing Puzzle	33
Gone	34
I Cry	36
Man	37
All I Think About is You	39
Tree of Love	40
Ms. Lucy	42
Priority	43
False Smiles	45
Collective Forever	47
A Short Look at Her Picture	49
In Love with a Poet	51
Cold Nights	53
Depress Tears	54
In Another World	56
What If's	58
Love Virus	59
I Found Myself	61

Last Night Eyes 63

God Knows 64

Crashed 66

Lonely Nights... 67

Distant Heart 69

Dear Love... 70

A Dimmed Moon 71

Pillow Talk 72

Prayer of Love.. 74

Trust 76

Treason of the Heart.. 77

I've Waited... 78

Return of an Arrow 79

Candy Kisses.. 80

Dreams to Nightmares 81

A Dream from the Moon... 83

I Smiled.. 85

Dear Possibility.. 86

My Eyes are Hurting.. 87

Dreams of Love.. 89

Battles 90

Fallen Leaf 92

My Heart 93

To Hold You	94
Beautiful	96
Love Again	97
Lost	98
Constant Prayer	99

Heart of Concrete

Have you ever had someone walk through you?

Then they stop at your heart and made love to it

To only crack it, to where you are internally bleeding

My eyes are crying red bricks

The foundation of my soul is crumbling

Left my spirit without the roots to rebuild my heart

I don't want to be forever shattered

Should I let another walk through me again?

Allow her to stop at my heart again so she can make love?

My heart is so fragile that another crack can give me a heart attack

Having my eyes crying again

Hopefully my tears will be shining bricks

Knowing she will stop at my heart and not only make love to it

She will help build it back to love again

Death of a Gentleman

There were many moons that capture the nights as he tries to understand

His heart no longer wants to love anyone

He lost faith in love that he decided to just exist in the world of romance

In his leisure time the only thing that he does is shelter his soul

The ability to connect to another has long gone

No more tears can form in his eyes so the hurt is hidden by smiles

Majority of the music he plays are saddened by the lyrics of songs

Tonight his thoughts consume his mind

His frustrations got the best of him that the anger inside begins to come out of his spirit

Why do this keep happening?

I'm tired of the hurt and pain as his voice sounds off like a trumpet

Then the clouds slowly hide the glow of the moon

It's a night to remember that he's exhausted from the overthinking

He lay under the covers with redness of the eyes but no tears formed

Hoping he would just fall asleep and rest his mind

Tomorrow he may have better reasoning to why hurt made love to his heart

Black Cloud

My heart is dark

The night becomes content with pain

No light can shine through the abyss of sorrow

It's like a raven pretends to be cupid

Lightning strikes the foundation of my peace

The thunder roars like lions speaking through the Serengeti

My heart is dark

The screams of my cries waters the inconsistency of my thoughts

Many roots are confused by the hurt that they form trees with no branches

I'm silent by the instability of the earth

The wind blows my discomfort

Will the sun appear to shine my heart?

A Jazzy Thought

As I sat I kind of overwhelm myself

My thoughts became stagnant to where I felt confused

It seems as though my soul was being used

I didn't know what to do

I decided to play a little jazz

Then i allowed the horns to make love to the sounds of the saxophone

My spirit became calmed that my thoughts started to roam

Every word created a rhythm like the piano

It was like my mind was playing a song without a singer

I need to express these feelings

I have no clue how to let go of my thoughts

Humming sounds manifested my heart

Then the slow melodies of my soul took control

I'm expressing myself to where the calmness of my heart starts to sing

I fell in love with myself and my soul invented this everlasting tune

I Just Made Love to You Invisibly

It was a night where you cross my mind numerous times

I wanted you close to my heart to where I needed to express my love

Then you appeared right in front of me, but no one would understand

I begin to light some candles then I rubbed your face

I can't conceal these emotions anymore

I slowly kiss your lips gently and softly

I want you to be secure in my arms as I protect your feelings

My lips slowly peck your neck as my hands rubbed you with a purpose

Then your moans created an aura of passion

Every kiss I can feel your energy as you enter my soul

Then I gradually walked you into my room

We look each other nervously in one another eyes as we took our clothes off

The thought of making love to you brings out an enchanting moment

I took a step back to admire your beauty

Then I calmly kiss your forehead as I lay you down on your back

Our kisses are getting stronger

This intimacy is really getting intense

I can feel the chemistry as I go deeper inside you

It's like the passion is connecting us as one

Your moans, my moans

Your kisses, my kisses

Your touch, my touch

I can feel a storm

The rain is flooding my earth

Your moans get louder

My body creates thunder

Then lightning strikes my spine

Our bodies invented an orgasm that is disguised by the speculation of love

A Seasonal Purpose

A knife stabs my soul and left me bleeding out

My subconscious start praying for my soul

Not knowing my conscious left my spirit to die

I'm bleeding all over my internal emotions

I'm slowly dying from the pain that was left from silent killers

Every minute without help is leaving me to succumb to my everlasting departure

My eyes are closing and my breath is coming to an end

It's a shame my life will end painless but shameless

Here lies a man who gave his sentiments to others

Not knowing his demise will be alone away from the roses he never got

Then my eyes finally closed to not breathe ever again

My life was written but it wasn't over

That was the end of the chapter of pain and now God wrote another story

I'm reincarnated into a passionate soul

My eyes open to a beautiful spirit and my subconscious was reborn

My conscious made love to my soul

Here's where life begins again, and I'm devoted to myself

The love that bleeds in my heart creates an aura of peace

I'm forever happy knowing my seasons had its reasons which
gave me a lifetime of tranquility

A Destroyed Promise

She was the sunlight in my life then as the days got closer to the moon purpose

The wind begins to howl deceitful clues

Truth started to reveal itself as my thoughts begin to ask questions

I can feel the temperature of my spirit shifts

Something doesn't feel right about how my body is responding to the lies

It feels like a tornado came into my heart and caused so much destruction

I can feel the thunder pounding against my chest as i worried about the damage

This everlasting pain is hurting me and my soul will need consistent construction

The agony from knowing the possibility of love has died causes a hurricane from my eyes

My face is flooded from the hurt and confusion from the clouds of her intentions

I need to find shelter from this storm of dishonesty

How could this happen when I was vulnerable and genuine?

The devastation has left me rebuilding my life again so I can prepare for another promise

Phenomenal Soul

It was a confused night to where I was alone once again

Then I begin to think about this special woman

It's like a distant connection

She stays on my mind with her remarkable energy

Who is this special woman that keeps my eyes on her?

Then I decided to get down and pray to God for guidance

I ask him to deliver this queen to my spirit

I wanted her to secure my heart with peace

As I got up from my prayer I begin to lay down

I was a little exhausted from the ordeal

Then I slowly close my eyes after I saw her face

I fell into a deep sleep not knowing God was talking to me

As he was molding her, I was in my dream visualizing her

He said son she's full of grace with a pleasing aura

Her heart is full of love and devotion

Will you respect her tenderness and passion that she possesses?

As I begin to wake I notice I had tears in my eyes

My heart felt full and it wasn't cold

I will continue to pray that God will send me this phenomenal soul

A Thoughtful Date

I spent many nights wondering why I sit alone at this table

Ordering food hoping you were sitting across from me

A beautiful creation from the clay that God molded from

I'm humble in my approach so you can see this gentleman

I hope she understands my thoughts and reasoning

I don't mean any disrespect, but I do mean my intentions are genuine

She's a friend, associate or whatever the title can be

But I know she have remarkable energy

It's the smile that makes me pause in the moment

I can appreciate her presence as she walks through my mind

Maybe it's her eyes that seems mysterious

Her physical frame is picture perfect

All those qualities I wish was sitting across the table

Then I order a glass of wine to soothe my nerves

Listening to her voice as she commands my heart

I'm mesmerized by the opportunity to feast as I want her near me

Sir are you finish ordering your food?

Wow how could I get lost in that split second
A slight chuckle as I replied
Yes I am as I snapped out of that day dream

Lifeless Love

I started to daydream in the middle of the night

Then I saw the moon disappear behind the clouds

My thoughts cringed from the idea of loving again

Eventually saddens consumes my heart to where my tears are afraid to run

I'm disappointed by the opportunity to be happy when I can't trust your heart.

I can't take another broken and shattered moment

My inability to put the pieces back together is overwhelming

I wouldn't know where to start

So I'll protect the blood flow as it beats for my life and not for love

Ear Trumpet

I've been spending numerous hours wondering why my eyes are in pain

When the inside of my ears is playing sounds that's confusing me

My heart is broken but the T has vanished from the reality

The sounds of the trumpets are losing the rhythm of jazz

I haven't felt this much turmoil in a long time and now my nerves are raising

The vibrations of the truth set the tone for my feelings

Understanding the situation can cause a brief moment of reflecting

I can't surrender because of the inability to control a chapter in my life

The melody and harmony have absented moments, but I need
to audition for my role in rehabilitation

Wings

I flew across your heart like an eagle

Then I landed on your heart

Our journey begins today

The love I have for you created a space of forever Will you

fly to forever with me?

Place your wings on my wings

Let's take off to a place of eternity

That way when we get there, we will land together with peace and love

A Warm Jamaican Moment

When I'm with you I'm stuck in the moment to where the clouds have no meaning

Even the moon disappears from the opportunity to shine on us

That's because you have a spiritual glow that brightens up our future

At one point in time your eyes told me your life story and the birds were chirping but there was no sound

It was like life was at a pause so I could fall in love again

Your touch was communicating to my soul that you are walking peace

That radiant smile gave me confirmation from God that you are one of his most precious creations

Your skin was smooth and silky when we embrace each other with a warm hug

Then something went wrong to where I could hear the birds chirping and the clouds have a meaningful purpose

The reality sets in that the moment of love was a dream that can come true in due time

Sage

I need you more than ever now because these storms are coming

I can feel they will produce pain and negativity

My soul needs protection from the spiritual evils that's trying to consume my balance

The vibration in my thoughts wants to connect to the planet Venus

Can this disrespectful imitating God control my ability to create positive rhythm?

I need that powerful soothing wind to blow that destructive energetic being to a place of mortality

My principles will decipher the cause and effect that's forming a sense of polarity

I need fire to make love to you so your scent will release a divine pheromone

Her

It's her

The sound of the cranking when the rollercoaster goes up

That excitement of knowing she about to be a thrill for me

It's her

The thoughts of her on my mind that my boss tell me to go home because I can't focus on my work

She can confuse me and keep me in tune at the same time

It's her

The taste of her skin quenches my taste buds and fulfilled my appetite

Her touch is like the sand by the shoreline of the ocean

She's the reasons I'm happy and my heart is calm

Can she exist for me one day?

Will she appear in my reality?

It's her

Who I'm destined to spend my forever with, but can God create her because these dreams are making me anxious

A Perfect DAY

I can appreciate a moment where I froze in time wondering if I'm on her mind

Then I closed my eyes to visualize her beauty that hypnotized my heart

She's special like a rose in a vase filled with water

Her growth produces an aura of commitment to success

I wanted to hold her hand and whisper compliments into her ears as she smiles

This woman was created by God specifically to be a strong black queen that inspires kings to lead

I'm in love with her ability to motivate me to where all my goals are accomplished

Then I snap out of that tranced to be overwhelmed knowing she's not there, but her presence is still flowing through my soul

This day was special because I expressed my heart to her and cupid shot a forever friendship inside my spirit

One Night Understand

It was one night full of many surprises

Our eyes connected to where we both smile every time we glance at one another You should see her beauty

Her body was commanding the entire room

All I could think about is my hands all over her body

Then I wonder what was she thinking when her eyes were upon me

What are her thoughts when regarding me?

I decided to walk closer to her to see how she would react to my presence

She gave me a smile and touch my fingers with this spontaneous look in her eyes

Then I decided to ask her what we're her thoughts when she glance

She stated I'm thinking the same thoughts you are having so what are you thinking now after me saying that?

I replied saying I'm open to take her somewhere she never been before

Then she stood up and said follow me as she slowly walks to the back room

My words led the decision to leave what we about to do in this place of ecstasy

Moments of passion felt like I knew her soil that captures my spiritual roots

After emotions was released from the storm that was created by the chemistry of our eyes

We walk back to our beginning positions then we glanced at one another with a smile

I'm wondering what she is thinking, and her look stated she was wondering the same about me

Then I stood up and walk her way to pass her to exit this occasion

I stop and place my hands on her shoulders and whisper have a great evening

Then she kisses me on my cheek and stated may God bless you

A Deep Cleaning

I wonder what's on her mind when she walks pass me

She seems like she's in a deep thought

I don't want to bother her but I want to figure her out

Then she proceeded to add the bleach to the water

Giving a scent of cleansing from the aroma

She's so beautiful but I can feel something deep inside maybe hurting

Then I visualized her sweeping her pain away making sure all the dirt is gone

So I watch her from a far giving her the space she may need

I just hope she sanitized her soul from all the pain she may have endured

I want to know more about her to where I can get closer to her new beginnings

Then she starts to mop and every time the motion goes left to right

It's like she's purifying all the agony and grief

I just pray her spirit is calm and clear from all the passed blemishes that may have caused any trauma

Table

I never felt this nervous to meet someone who gives me goosebumps

This is a moment that brings so much anxiety

My right hand is shaking so bad I got to get a grasp on this feeling

Then she walked in which made my left-hand starts shaking

I stood up to greet her with the scent from the cologne I picked out just for her

Our smiles connected as my hands start to calm down

At this moment I'm in a romantic trance

Then I pulled her chair out showing her I am a gentleman

I can't stop telling myself how beautiful she is with that red dress on

Death of a Poet

The race is over

I slowed down so others can have their chance

Many don't understand

This is my heart bleeding for answers

My tears have tears

They run the down my face from the pain inside

It's like my words are afraid to speak

So I yelled deep inside my mental cave

All I hear is the bats flying across the sky

I can only vision the clouds but then they turn dark

The sun lost its power to where the earth forgot its purpose

I have no more reason to run anymore

The battle of expression was therapeutic

My chapter is complete

The paragraphs have no more sentences

It's time for the index of my soulful book to end

I gave my pen everything

It can't bleed the torment anymore

I placed a band aid on my notebook

Dark Light

I can feel the thunder inside my mind

It's like a storm is forming with every thought I'm having

The sun that shines positive energy is dimming

Each cloud has its own storms

I can't think

I can't concentrate

It's like the nouns and verbs are fighting

It's an explosion from every sentence

I'm lost inside a tsunami

The rain is pouring down my cheeks

I have a puddle on my chest and when i look down

All the tears have sadness

Why is the pain happening to me?

I can't breathe properly

I have no spiritual shelter

The storm is getting worse

My speech is quiet

I can't yell for help

Where's the sun at?

I need brighter days

Can this be a moment of confusion?

God why is my soul hurting when all i want is better?

I kneel to your invisible feet

I submit my sorrow to you

Please take this pain away

Grant me the love and peace I need

I'm obedient

As I close my eyes and allow the storm to run its course

I'll be patient and when my eyes open then I'll know my day will be brighter

Heaven Sent

God sent you to me

It felt like a dream came true

That spontaneous moment like we supposed to be here

A choice we both made to share each other's hearts

You are a breath of fresh air that consumes my lungs with love

It was like you were the message in the bottle floating to my soul

As I open this emotional note

It read all the things god has written for his instructions

I will obey his commands to do right by you

These are the times I don't want much

All I need is your heart speaking to me

You are telling me your soul is my home

Then I'll explain to you my spirit was built for you to live

My arms spreads like an angel that wants to embrace you

Take you on a flight of love

The sky will be a place of tranquility that we can share as one When it's time to land we will glide into forever

Lay

If I could lay one more night with you, I would cuddle all night

Hold you close to my heart so you can feel my love for you

Then you will turn your face around and kiss me

Now we can lay in peace knowing you are secured in the arms of a king

I'm protecting my queen from anything harmful

Her dreams will force any nightmares to leave her spirit

We are connected by God and the angels respect our bond

When the morning come, we will be well rested

Forgive

Can you forgive my moment?

It wasn't my intentions

My agenda is to learn your soul

Don't put me in love detention

You are special to me

In this short time, you consume my thoughts

Your smile is like the sun in the morning

Communication with you is like a cup of tea

Your questions stimulate my mind

You laying on my chest is where you should be

Take your time and know my sincerity is real

I was so comfortable with your spirit

My heart is pure and this how genuinely how I feel

Missing Puzzle

These thoughts are fighting each other

My verbs won't allow the adjectives to create a phrase

I'm afraid

I fear these headaches won't stop

Why won't the confusion of my mind don't go away?

It's like at times my peace doesn't have the energy to fight

My mental structure is starting to destruct

I'm lost in my own logic to where I can't understand the reasoning

I can hear the yelling from all the words causing an altercation

There's no tranquility in my spiritual chapter

Every paragraph in my soul dies

Gone

You left me looking into the mirror facing my doubts

I have no confidence to move forward

This pain took my breath away

My heart is shattered to where all the pieces scattered

I'm blinded by the hurt that I can't find any pieces

My destiny took a turn for the worse

Why did you leave me in a space of chaos?

I'm so hurt

This a love curse

These tears are crying and screaming for help

Every beat in my heart starts to melt

I'm feeling destruction within my soul

It's like I have no one

A thought of being left in the cold

I can't understand

Where do I go from here?

I don't want a lifetime of fear

This pain is so severe

I'm reaching my hands out for some comfort

Living in a world of contentment is not my life

My passion for love won't let me stay in a space if uncertainty.

I Cry

I cried so hard it felt like a thunderstorm was forming inside of me

My anxiety was beginning to flare up

The tears were rolling down my cheek so slowly

I'm so sad and full of emotions

My heart is racing rapidly

Then more tears start to create puddles around my foot

The floor is a river with powerful waves

My eyes are burning with sorrowful reasoning

It seems like my world is crashing and the moon don't exist

Majority of my thoughts feels like everything i do ends with a intense concern

I need to calm down and try to rest

I'm mentally exhausted from the trauma of my past

The only way my future will be better if i change my thoughts and have closure

Man

The genesis

God created me

Place his hands into the world and molded me

A beautiful being

Spirituality consumes my spirit

My smile is radiant like the sun rays

I have eyes keen like an eagle

The strength comes from my ancestor's defeat

They live through my blood

I'm a fighter

Overcame many obstacles

The air is the longevity of my truth

I can taste the fruits that's harvest from my hard work

I am man

The ability to lead

A brain full of thoughts in which some overcomes him

Others constitutes principles

I have a mission to become gods glory

To Leave a legacy that tell my story

Gratitude inside my soul makes love to the sincerity of my vitality

I am a man

There's no perfection on my journey

My purpose is unique because I was taught the meaning of life

All I Think About is You

All I think about is you and how my heart touches your soul

It's like the sun is kissing the river as it flows into a lake

I haven't felt this way in a long time

The birds are chirping as the wind blows the leaves on the branches

I just want to hear your voice as your words penetrate my mind

Telling my you miss me and can't wait to see me again

This is the feeling I've been wanting for a long time

It's like I'm lost in love from the special moments we share

I just can't stop thinking about you

Tree of Love

On this dreadful night

I can see the leaves covering the ground

The wind is blowing making the trees talk

All I do is think about you

It feels like my heart wants to meet yours

I'm constantly looking out the window waiting for cupid to appear

Will he have the perfect arrow?

When it comes to me, he's been missing the target

I just want to stare into your eyes and start to read your story

Do you have a chapter you writing for me to be a part of your life?

What does your heart say when my energy communicates to you?

Cupid is running late, and it seems like I'm only here for a reason

Maybe the season was changing

Then the wind blows harder and stronger

I can hear the whistling from the air trying to tell me something

It's probably telling me the trees lost it chance but when this season is over

Then the leaves will reappear where it's destined to be

Ms. Lucy

It was a strange night

I wanted to rest my head but then I realized God had a plan for me

It was to meet this special woman who created a moment

She seems secluded from her thoughts as she smiles at me

I wonder what words was recited in her mind

Then she catered to my taste buds Who is Ms. Lucy?

What motivates her to be a positive spirit?

Then she opens up her heart about the loss of her brother

She didn't know I lost my brother

Two people that told us to be better

I guess it was the mild weather as I sip on her love that she poured in my drink

Thank you Ms. Lucy, because not only that you were amazing, but you helped my depression

Priority

I never been this hurt to where my heart froze

It died one night where I felt the warmth was leaving

Every beat got slower and slower

My blood pressure got lower and lower

The love in my heart passed away

I lost the ability to secure another

Why did you do this to me?

Left me confuse from the truth my eyes endured

I'm breathless laying in my bed

My tears are raining pain on my heart as I succumb to these wounds

I'm so hurt

I'm shattered

I'm disappointed

A man who had the endurance to win the race of love

All I can see is cupid flying away with the arrow he shot into my heart

Here lies a man who wanted love

A man who was destined to be the beat of your heart

Only future thoughts of the what ifs will absorb you
My understanding of knowing love died inside of my spirit

False Smiles

There's pain behind those smiles

Your melancholy attitude is wearing on your sleeve

Do you pray for the pain to leave?

Instead, your weakness in your mind takes over with greed

The power of being relevant makes you happy

Then you go home and take off the mask to be depressed

Using social media as a way to suppress those feelings

Your smile is not radiant

It looks like a gloomy cold day in Chicago

Your eyes are telling the story that you are not happy

The pain you live with have a cure, but you choose to ignore it

The mirror you look into don't have a reflection

Self-love is the antidote to your misery

Social media and putting others down is your deflection

Your tears have tears because you are so hurt

Every time you grin there's a crack in your face

The energy is shown that you aren't happy in your own space
These same people who you are trying to impress are smiling like you

A coalition of unhappiness

A cult of misery

Take the time to change your mindset so you can change how you feel

It's time to be ecstatic to produce positive energy

Only a genuine humble soul can smile respectfully

Collective Forever

I want to love you

Place my heart into your soul

You place your heart into mines

We become one

Then we can create a future forever

Making love to every weather

You are my infinite season

The stars are the peace

The moon is the happiness

The sun is the coffee to our day

I want to love you

Become the period to your sentence

You are the question mark to my thoughts

We have the chemistry that can spark

The universe never lies

You will forever be the light to my dark

I fell in love with you the first day

It was like a summer day when I saw your smile

Your glow was the cure to the gloomy moments I was having

The days we spent together and the night I laid with you
It felt like a war cup of tea with lavender
I was at peace in your arms
You seem like serenity was holding you
Our spirits were making love while we were sleep
When we woke up from a dream
We knew we had tranquility
The vision of loving you became a reality
I will never stop loving the idea of being forever happy

A Short Look at Her Picture

I stared at her picture to where I feel like I know her

Every blink in my eyes I vision moments spending time with her

I can see her past while looking at her present

Who is this beautiful mysterious woman?

Can I trust her with my present and my future?

I believe I found peace while looking into her eyes

Her skin glows like the sun rays shining on the lake

Her hair is like the trees full of life to where the roots show her ancestry

This woman body resembles the queen commanding respect

Will I ever get a chance to meet this woman?

I want to tell her my many thoughts

Excuse me sir

Yes, I replied

You are holding up the line

I had to snap out of this trance

Didn't know I fell in love with her beauty
She was picture perfect
Can't believe she captured my attention
While someone captured her and place her in a frame

In Love with a Poet

When i see her all that comes to me are words
Her voice was like a moment of calmness
She wrote verses on my heart
Not the typical roses are reds
It more like the ability is she could
You know be in my world
Me in her world
Creating a universal relationship
Her rhythm gives me chills down my spine
A beautiful woman that makes me juggle words that rhyme
I never stop thinking about her
A goddess of a woman
Every line is like perfection
Her eyes are like the notepad waiting for my pen
A combination of respect when I begin to write
Every word she has written froze my thoughts
She's the syllables of the words I'm thinking
My aura changes every time I see her face
That beautiful chocolate queen

With a smile that brightens up my space

Her energy has frequencies that seems to come from a place of love

Why can't she see my pen is bleeding for her heart?

I wish I could erase past transgressions

I can only hope she can see the sincerity of my soul

The one poet who I would love to recite to forever

Cold Nights

Those cold nights come

I embrace them every chance I get

I'm protected by allowing the chill to secure my heart

My thoughts consume my soul

No other being will get close to my rhythm

No smiles

No love

Disrespectful auras

I don't need reasoning

Even explanation fell asleep

Shallow minds weren't deep

Only being exile from the wicked ones guarded my spirit

These cold nights begin to warm up

I lost so much that this pain will yield into a space of balanced

Love took a vacation

Death left my thoughts so I'm alive

My character and morals are intimate

Peace solidifies my purpose

Depress Tears

Those nights were brutal I
found myself depress from
the stress
Nothing matters but falling asleep
Just laying in the bed secluded from the world
I can't believe I cried so long that my pillow was soak
It was drench in pain
All my dreams were nightmares of me drowning in my shame
My heart has died and resurrected numerous times
Even the sheep was jumping for me to count
They grazed in a state of melancholy
All I can do is cry
These tears are so sad
My eyes are burning
I'm so hurt that I'm yearning
Why can't I stop crying?
Happiness is homeless from
My heart
I just feel lost

It's like I'm frozen in a silent place

All I have is these thoughts that consumes my mind

My days are like a dreadful drive through hell

I need to rest

Fill this emptiness

I feel like I'm dying

I'm so ashamed of myself

What can I do?

I can't stop this crying

In Another World

We would be happy

Secluded in a place where only our lives would show

No judgment would consume our moment

We would make love slowly as the moon turns into the sun

You would be my heart

I would love your soul

I will take a vow to love you for better and worse

In another world

You would love me unconditionally

Our families would blend together as one

You will love my heart

Then you would love my soul

Do you take me to be your lawful forever?

Many days would be more than a dream

So many nights the stars will calm our nights

Our dedication to love is what keeps us consistent

Life would be the mold that god created

Then reality sets in drastically

In this world

We love one another

Only to not have each other

What If's

Many days I daydream wishing you were sitting in front of me

I'm in love with the possibility

The thoughts of you having a picnic with me gives me stability

My heart is warm when I'm near you

As the day goes on all I can do is think of you and me

A mental vision is so tunnel because you are all i see

You remind me of a moment watching a parade

Every act brings me so much joy

Then the sun starts to set which lets me know this dream will end

The tunnel vision because very clear

The moon will tell me about my place in your life

As God lay me down to sleep

I pray for jumping hearts

All I got was a wet pillow from the tears

At least I got the sun shining but I can see many clouds

My daydream becomes a nightmare as I think of loving you forever

Love Virus

It was a dark night just laying in my bed

Many thoughts took over my mind

I lost the possibility of loving you again

My heart was deleted from your love

You left me singing love songs that created my love for you

These tears are felt in the universe to where someone is crying from hurt

Pain has become a virus and cupid was sick from the symptoms

I have no one to shoot an arrow in the sky in hopes to Pierce her soul

It's like loving you gave me chills

My body aches from the consistent agony

I'm starting to experience a tremendous headache

Shortness of breath is starting to give anxiety

Fatigue weakens my ability to move forward

This virus call love has affected many in different ways

So tonight, I need a cure so I can get well

It's like I'm under a broken love spell

I'm sick

I'm feeling pain
It's like I'm dying
The agony and discomfort
I can't stop crying
Tonight, has broken my will
All I can do is doze off and hopefully when I wake
The possibility has become a reality

I Found Myself

It's my time

My moment of truth

My visions became the focal point of my life

I decided to respect my journey

These are the events that are critical to my balance

Peace became still when the pain was released to God

The bitterness that consumed my spirit was an emotional mess

I lived for the hurt people hurt people mindset

The change that was coming was my calling

God answered many cries

These tears had meaning

Each drop was an event that I was a part of

Then The healing started today

The therapy was a major key to the peace I needed inside my soul

I can admit that anger was the love of my life

Many more tears told the story of past miscues

Only blaming myself is the first step to repairing my soul

I'm ascending to a place of tranquility

My growth is the reward from the lessons that were learned

I personally won't let myself down again

The love I have within are the principles I will protect forever

Last Night Eyes

I was frozen in time to where I was lost in your eyes

My heart was shedding tears inside

And this particular moment anxiety took control of my soul

Your eyes connected and my vibration was shock

I couldn't focus because my mind was racing leaving me to overthink

I was too afraid to speak freely

You have this authority over me

I'm spiritually speechless

Then I got lost in your eyes from the time you walk in

This the moment I've been waiting for

Having some sort of peace that became still every time you blink

My heart begins to melt like butter

It's like I'm on a cloud in harmony secluded in the blue sky

Your love penetrated the confusion that was instilled inside my body

The mood for the rest of the evening is set to be full of tranquility

God Knows

We all have weaknesses

The inability to control the moments

Our purpose has so many reasons, but our journey has been written

Letting go is the hardest thing to do

The tears overflow your face

Every tear has a meaning

Pain

Death

Heartbreak

Then we put our all in our faith

They are the words from God that gives us hope

The scriptures with instructions of life

We have to be patient

How can we?

The tears continue to control the moments

All we can do now is pray

Pleading with God for the ultimate reassurance

Gods knows because he created the purpose for our journey

You are strong

Only you can dig deep inside your soul

Sacrifice the torture that consumes your conscience

Allow God to ease your pain with comfort

Peace will be still inside your heart so you can defeat all your
worries

Crashed

Destiny failed to execute its purpose

Even the moon hid behind the clouds

Many stars stayed far away

The sun only shined at a particular place

Love remained distant from the ability to live inside one's heart

Why can't life be so simple?

The moments where the breeze can calm souls

To where the birds are chirping from the trees

How the hummingbirds can fly into flowers

The way the clouds can produce showers

Visions of perfection from every wave

The boats sailed across the ocean

It's the opportunity to where the water kisses the shoreline

Can lust resurrect itself into love?

Will cupid shoot an arrow that can strike sincere hearts?

The fact that destiny may have failed but everyday someone has a chance to fulfill their purpose

Lonely Nights

These are the hardest times

Where life tends to pause so you can't think

Used your time to reflect

Place your thoughts inside your heart

Your soul begins to speak

My intentions aren't going to be frozen

This emptiness has consumed my life

It's like can't function

I can't believe isolation is what i have chosen

Compassion is the only thing that motivates me

Lying here lost inside my spirit

Visualizing moments of clarity

Why do my pillow cry at night?

Can these tears reverse back inside my eyes?

Then flashes of love making crosses my mind

I'm stuck trying to figure out the reasoning of being companionless

Suddenly romance walked out of my life and begin to date another soul

Once again I feel broken and shattered

These are the nights I'm lost but my story hasn't been told

Can love navigate back into my life?

Will happiness declare peace to the chaos that triggers my agony?

These lonely nights can't haunt forever hopefully one day companionship will have a purpose in my expedition to love

Distant Heart

My tears are broken

They are running down my face, but my heart is shattered

Confusion has placed a moment inside my mind

The closure I require froze as communication begins

Is this going to be another time of disappointment?

These thoughts took my heart and implanted hope

I'm distant from reality knowing my purpose ended

I can't believe my love will be stranded as stagnation put a halt to my happiness

My destiny is not fulfilled

I have an empty soul because I only have you from a distance

You are the missing piece to the puzzle of evermore

Dear Love

I need you

No moment goes by without a thought of you

Then I realize you have hurt me

Put me in situation to where it's times where I didn't care about you

My feelings weren't valid

You took me for granted

Everything you said to me wasn't true

Why me?

You can have anybody, but you want me

I can feel the wind blow stability into my spirit

Then occasionally I have no feelings

It leaves numbness to devour every little bit of belief I have for you

Please understand I have no room for an emotional rollercoaster

My healing gave me an opportunity to rehabilitate my heart and soul I do love you

These feelings are genuine

Sincerely your forever love

A Dimmed Moon

It was a warm spring night as I look into the sky

I witness darkness with a dimmed ray

The moon was afraid to come outside

Only the stars had a slight glare

The night wasn't calmed

Every visible cloud tried to protect the moon from something

Even the branches on the trees were starting to move rapidly

The wind has anger that sends a fierce breeze

What's happening?

I can smell fear in the air

Then I look up at the sky again

Water starts to slowly kiss my face

Sadness took over the earth surface

Tonight, a storm begins to form

The moon forgot its purpose

Pillow Talk

Laying in this bed

Tears creates puddles on my pillows

My heart is broken by life

This soul of mines is full of love

Then I wonder what life would be like if I didn't have a past

The same past that others don't understand

God had a plan

Some say a calling

I didn't understand until I stuck between chaos and peace

My emotions get the best of me

I'm only human to the point where my flaws are my strengths

It's like many don't understand my purpose

Only a few can crack the surface

I'm hurt behind repair shattered like a falling vase

Hiding behind pain with smiles

Never thought being broken would haunt me forever

Pain lives in my bloodstream

My soul is detached from the world

I'm existing in a place of insecurity
I feel lost without a piece of soul
Missing the pieces to my forever puzzle
Why me?
Do I deserve this hurt?
Patience don't live inside of me anymore
I need answers
These questions cloud my brain
Why?
Someone tell me why
It's like I'm drowning in this puddle
Knowing my tears consumes my spirit

Prayer of Love

I prayed night after night

Hoping to fall in love again

Just wondering what stability feels like

Oh, father please grant me the peace of love

The ability to be vulnerable

I have so much passion inside that I want to unleash these emotions

Give another my heart and be free knowing she will receive my divine love

We can trust each other without the worries of distractions

As the sky is full of clouds

The birds chirping

The bond we created will be unbreakable

I'm devoted to the peace of love

I want to Have many moments to where my heart feels safe when I'm with her

Oh God I pray deep with sincerity to remove all the confusion from my life

I'm deserving of feeling warm inside

Please resurrect my soul

Give me another chance to love again

I'll take the oath of devotion

To forever dedicated my heart and soul to your creation of my spirit

I surrender my life to you father God

My patience is my courage to be ready for your blessings

It's you that cast out my sins because as I fall deep asleep

You will take my forever rib and place it inside of her

Then I will wake one day knowing your prophecy for me is fulfilled

Trust

When I'm alone i can feel darkness inside my soul

I walk through my mind lost and enslaved by my thoughts

I'm vulnerable to pain to where suffering begins to kiss my spirit

Every thought sounds like bats are flying across the top of a cave

The avenue to peace seems like a lifetime journey

Can tonight be a night of impairment?

I can't remove this discomfort from my body

I don't have the answers that holds my consciousness captive

Then I visualized some relief from a voice that soothed the inner part of my heart

My friend appeared in my ears reassuring me life is precious

Have strength and never lose hope

God have all the answers just believe in your faith

Tomorrow will bring you serenity and patience

Treason of the Heart

I never been this hurt and still loved you at the same time

It's like I'm confused wondering why the sun lost its shine

You disrespected my ability to lived

I can't function without the constant reminder of my heart being still

Why did you break the oath of love?

Then you secluded yourself into the arms of another

I can't melt this pain inside my heart

All I can do is visualize you with your deceitful lover

How could you show dishonor?

I'm broken internally by the outcome of my soul

Forgiveness has vacated any possibility

You have hurt me beyond any repair

My rib was placed in your body and now it's being replaced I lost my purpose for love when love damaged my spirit.

I've Waited

My love for you is so strong that I will wait forever for you

I'm committed to your soul

When the blizzard comes and covers the ground with snow

I will wait until you shovel my heart from under the frost

You complete the goal of love for me

Every thunderstorm I feel safe knowing you are the umbrella to my soul

Then I will wait again

Wondering will you appear in my dreams

Would prayers bring you closer to me?

I'm writing a love letter then I will place it in a bottle

Maybe the ocean will have a different outcome knowing the waves took my words to your heart Should I continue to wait?

Place my love for you on hold

I can't make love to another

I'm dedicated to the possibility of evermore

Return of an Arrow

I seen cupid fly across the sky with a look of concerned

He seems like he was looking for someone

He stops on top of me and then I felt a sharp pain in my chest

Cupid took his arrow back from inside my heart

I was left in pain feeling like I was having a heart attack

The confusion from not knowing why have me in a state of distress

I feel like I'm dying inside without any answers

This agony from the pain is too much to bear

Why would he leave me without the feeling of love?

Then he appeared again to explain why he took back my ability to love

He stated my soulmate had a change of heart

Her love for me was a season

He said it's time for me to heal from my injuries

I'm left with forever pain and now I'm on the waiting list of love

Candy Kisses

You had me at hello to where after I walked into your life I didn't want to leave

My heart is warm and melting every time your eyes mysteriously glare at me

This is a feeling of peace knowing your hands secures my soul

Then my mind shifted thinking about your lips

Each kiss tells a story on how much you love me

I can feel your energy with every peck

I'm addicted to your vibe

It's like I'm overwhelmed by not having you near

My lips feel alone waiting for the opportunity

The possibility of making love from a taste of your tongue

I go into a state of hypnosis

A feeling of passion consumes my soul after my passionate diagnosis

It's like a battle I'm fighting between love and lust

The power you have over me is stimulating

I'm stuck in your web, but I surrender my spirit to you knowing we have trust

Dreams to Nightmares

I fell asleep many nights afraid not knowing if the demons will march in my thoughts like a parade

It's a scary charade how the devil can participate in your mind

I pray before I closed my eyes not knowing the outcome of my visions

These past missions I use to do from seeing humans shock not knowing tonight maybe their last

The only thing they can remember is the blast but then it went fast

Death consumes the night to where the sirens were louder than the wolves roar

Maybe the visual of me being hurt by another because my spirit was vulnerable

Karma made love to my soul and telling me my time is now

I lost so many people but this one hurts the most because a soulmate died in the thoughts of my charisma

 She left me bleeding inside full of pain and emptiness

It's like a head on collision where I'm dying on the concrete probably where another was drunk in love

Maybe the zipper that closed the body bag as she passes to another world

My love gone forever and all I have is the memories of her teachings

Who will say a prayer for the man who wants love?

Can a voice appear from the sky?

Will the angels bring the messages from God as the moon hides behind the clouds?

It's a cold world full of confusion and hate but I remain hopeful

Gratification went on a vacation and made love to sincerity

I died tonight like every night when my eyes closed

Wondering how the devil can leave me alone so I can rest peacefully

I'm eager to see what the outcome of my thoughts that comes from the trauma of no guidance

I just want to count sheep and hearts versus fire and pitchforks

My destiny is stagnant from not healing from the past, but my present is contagious

Can someone pray for me but not just for me?

Help me defeat the demons that consumes my dreams

All I want you to do is sleep

A Dream from the Moon

It was a calm night taking a long walk around the world

She captured my thought process to where I'm feeling stimulated

I paused trying to figure out the signs of a future

Then the nouns begin to create sentences inside my heart

My spirit is the book of love as her voice soothes my chapters

Abruptly I got lost inside my mind afraid of the outcome

What if she's a short-term distraction?

It's something about her that's forcing this attraction

At this moment the moon established a relationship with my emotions

I'm frozen in time trying to count the sheep as I dreamed of her intentions

Suddenly cupid flew across the sky but so far nothing was mentioned

All the pain inside her spirit needs time to heal but I hope it don't change how she feels

My purpose is to continue to show her my sincerity

As I woke up from a brisk sleep, I notice the moon was hidden behind the clouds

All at once I try to brace my feelings not knowing if she will hide behind her past transgressions

Only time will tell if the universe creates stars and form a timeless bond

I Smiled

Today I cried a few times wondering if God heard my cries

Then I realized the world don't revolve around me

So, I took a break from my thoughts and I'm humble myself

I understood my life have a purpose and my journey was molded by God

Then I smiled

Took my heart and created a moment of happiness

My tears reversed back into my eyes and I kept my tears inside my heart

Then God whisper to me, son I gave you life and within life you prosper

I cried but this time it was tears of joy

I smile today because I'm grateful but faithful to the fact I'm blessed from the opportunities of life

Dear Possibility

These are the moments that I wish you were here

Maybe vice versa just staring into your eyes

Wondering if I could read your thoughts when you look at me

Then I took a pause to figure out my emotions

I can't sleep because you have crossed my mind and stop in the middle of my consciousness

I'm frozen in the imagination of the moment

This point I'm trying to make is you have me intrigue by the way you make me feel

I haven't felt this way in a long time

It's like not seeing the stars and the moon together

It's been that long but tonight the sky is full of light

The thought of you calms the storms inside my soul

I can get some rest knowing the moon relaxed me and I know the sun will brighten my day

So as the night ends with a slight coldness in the air

I hope I will cross your mind and warm your spirit with reassurance

Sincerely a future opportunity

My Eyes are Hurting

I cried so many times that my eyes are hurting

My eyes are hurting

My eyes are hurting

I'm Losing my hydration because the pain won't leave my soul

My eyes are hurting

My eyes are hurting

The pain runs down my face forcing itself to create a puddle of agony

Then placing me in seclude position to make myself feel sadness

My eyes are hurting

My eyes are hurting

I can't seem to stop myself from flooding my spirit

These Waterfalls from within is giving me anxiety and i can feel a panic attack coming on

I'm lost in my thoughts of trying to figure out the puzzle of love

My strength is becoming weaker by the minute

I want the rain to stop and my soul needs an eternal umbrella

Why can't my eyes stop hurting?

I feel defeated when I thought I had control over my emotions

I pray my feelings can change and my heart can stop racing so fast

The finish line can be the end of my eyes hurting so the pain can turn into peace

Dreams of Love

I made love to you in my dreams

It was like I was counting hearts instead of sheep

I can feel the skin of your body touching my skin

We were connecting from the connection within

Your lips grasp my lips

Your tongue communicated your feelings for me

My hands caress the soft clay that God created

Our eyes were showed so much passion for one another

It felt like perfection on the grass in the garden of Eden

We are making love passionately

One soul is inside another soul and vice versa

I took your breath inside my spirit

We were so close together we became one

Then I can hear the sounds of us having an orgasm together

To realized it was my alarm clock and the dream was over

I can't wait to go back to sleep tonight knowing you will be waiting for me again

Battles

I'm a determined fighter

The strength comes from the support of my loved ones

The courage is my ability to tell my story without judgement

My testimony is my purpose to give back so I can help others

I battle PTSD and times I'm depress

I know it's a test

The anxiety turns into panic attacks which feels like a heart attack I'm a fighter

The Gemini inside of me is deeper than ying and yang

It's the fight between introvert and extrovert

I get silent at times to where I don't want people too close to me

I rather have the verbs and nouns in my thoughts as my friends

It's too many disappointments from humans that creates barriers

God knows my heart and my intentions

I have issues with my hearing at times to where the ringing is louder than the sound of words

Wearing hearing aids are the remedy to the ringing

I hide them from the world because I'm embarrassed

I'm a fighter

I don't talk to others because many don't understand my deep sacred feelings

Trying to trust others with my battles as they may fight their own is not my goals

My battles are apart me and at times they may overpower me

Then I realize the fight I have inside of me comes with the strength of my spirituality

Fallen Leaf

It was cold brisk afternoon and there was this leaf dangling from this weary branch

The wind had a slight attitude as the branch begins to shake rapidly

It seems like it was destined to fall to the ground

A similar feeling that my heart endured from sadness

Then the branch released the leaf as it slowly falls to its purpose

My thoughts of having closure from a previous situation so i released my emotions from them

Now the leaf kisses the dirt and laid in position of still

The pain that controls my soul is beginning to diminish

A leaf no longer has a relationship with the branch and my heart is single from the failed commitment

Hopefully the next leaf will have the opportunity to stay a little bit longer

My Heart

My heart is the love that I share with you

Your heart is the love that you share with me

We are connected by air

The air that's released from the lungs of destiny

Your breath blew into me with your intentions

My breath blew into you my ability to protect

I take this vow to secure your heart from lust

As I looked deep inside your eyes translating my reasoning

Your eyes nurtured my spirit with the warmth of care

My eternal love for you is endless

I found my forever purpose

It was the prayers that I recited to God begging for my rib to be removed

I want cupid to perform this operation of commitment

You are my heart when it beats rapidly from your touch

You are my heart that beats slow from the calmness of your soul.

Sincerely My Heart

To Hold You

During this time all you needed was a hug from me

It was a moment for you to get yourself back balance

Then I failed you

I took my selfishness and created disrespect towards you

My apologies comes from my heart because God knows it

Forgiveness is what I need but I know you need time to process my actions

During this time you needed an ear

A shoulder to cry on while your tears roll down my back

Your heart is tired and your spirit is exhausted

My apologies again come from the scriptures of refuge

You are worth the world

The moon has a place on its craters waiting for you to sit

Take your time to overlook the universe

I love you from the other crater looking at your sadness

I pledge allegiance to your soul that I'll do better

I also feel like I lost a part of my peace

Holding your hand and looking into your eyes as you read the words coming from my lips

My apologies is deeper than nouns and verbs
They are the composition of my spirit

Beautiful

Do you believe that a beautiful face can be equivalent to the sun?

I believe because her face is full of glow

She's so beautiful but not that arrogant type of beauty

Her beauty has humbleness and sincerity

God molded her from the clay with the power of his hands

It's like the sand by the shoreline

Her eyes are gracefully at peace

I wish they were glaring into mines as I lean closer

Her lips look soft as I want to kiss them

Then I pause to get out of my daydream

It felt like a long sleep

She has me hypnotized by her skin that have this cocoa butter gleam

Even during my glooming days

I can't wait to see the sun shining when she posts her picture

Love Again

If I could love you again I would but it would be different this time around

It would be moments of a slow pace, so I don't have to rush my love for you

When I'm rubbing your feet you would close your eyes knowing you have security from me

When I rub your legs so tight and firm you would know my care for you is important

As I lay you on your stomach and begin to rub your back

You will close your eyes again knowing that my love for you is how God wanted me to love you

That way when you open your eyes you would look me into my eyes

At that particular moment you will know my hands not only rubbed you but molded my forever fingerprints into your body

Lost

Winning with satisfaction is my goal but I feel I lost you

It's times where I know deep down in my roots of my soul it won't happen

I refuse to tell the universe my heart when it's about you

It's a confusing time

One minute I need to stop because my heart is so fragile

Within the hour my love for you gets so stronger that I walk on eggshells

I'm afraid of another broken heart

There's no guarantees with love

The possibilities are endless because my love is sincere

The same roots of my soul have this special place where you live

Many times I have to travel inside my spirit to stay in love with you

It's one of the best vacations I've been on in a long time

Then it's a place inside my mind where I know the outcome of this relationship

I will lose you to another and swallowing the sorrow of this pain is inevitable

Constant Prayer

As I kneeled down to the floor my head touches the ground

I beg and plea to God for your return to my heart

The conversation with the lord comes with many tears knowing I may have lost my soul mate

Then I heard a soft demanding voice that seemed to be on my shoulder

Is this you God?

What are your commands for my life?

I begin to place my head on the floor again discussing my reasoning for my decision to continue to pursue her

Then that same soft voice with an instrumental sound telling me to be patient and resilient to my feelings

I'm in a position of submission disclosing my thoughts on wanting her love again or will this be the end of a soul tie?

Her heart is secluded in another soul, but she has no choice but to love the moment she's in

Then I ended my prayer knowing I gave God and the universe my intentions for her

This the time in my life is where I got to stay strong and hopeful for my opportunity once again

Her heart is important to my heart

I value her so much but not able to express my feelings is a tough stance I have to take

Patience is a virtue and one day our connection will return

If not, I'll always cherish her and be a forever soul if she needs me to be

The Author

Mario Givens is an author of five poetry books in which The Love Notes being one of his best books he's written. He's born and currently lives in Chicago Illinois. He uses poetry to tell his story but also inspire others to have similar expressions. When not writing, he can be found at a stage play, museums, traveling and overall helping his community.

You can connect with Mario on Twitter or Instagram at @mariogivens or check out his website at
WWW.MARIOGIVENS.COM

www.ingramcontent.com/pod-product-compliance
Lightning Source LLC
Chambersburg PA
CBHW071147060526
44107CB00133B/342